NO I DON'T

HAVE A JOB

I'M JUST NOT CUT OUT TO BE AN EMPLOYEE

Rashad Shepherd

TABLE OF CONTENT

INTRODUCTION

The mere fact that you are reading this book right now confirms that, deep down inside you have that gut feeling that you are cut out to be more than just someone's employee. If you are feeling that way, then you are right my friend. You were not born to just pay bills and die, and you were not born to be controlled by some job and the system. The fact that you decided to read this book says a lot about you. I understand that everybody won't be A BOSS or THE BOSS, someone has to be the employee. Well, this book isn't for just someone, this book is for you. You don't even have to have plans to run or own a big company with hundreds or thousands of employees, but you should at least have plans to take control of your life. Someone like you shouldn't be settling for some job. You have too much potential and creativity. The world needs to see and hear about it. You should be investing in your ideas, pursuing your dreams and learning how to establish your own business or brand.

Can you imagine getting called into your boss's office unexpectedly and receiving the news that your job is about to be made redundant due to a financial recession or due to some long-term renovations? Can you imagine being fired for something like a complaint made against you by another colleague or getting fired for doing something that were not up to company or job standards? How would you feel? I'm certain that it would be a shocker for you. Some people would go in instant depress mode.

The question is, do you want to be a victim of such uncertainty? Do you want to be forced into making decisions about your life or do you want to freely decide what moves you want to make? It's time to be a boss and make your own decisions.

Mr. Social Media, marketing expert and entrepreneur Gary Vaynerchuk, the author of the books #AskGaryvee and Crush It, said that when you get to do what you want to do, you've won.

After 9 years, going from job to job not being able to fit in, adjust or get comfortable. I just knew it was finally time to live life my way. I honestly sucked at being an employee anyway. So, to avoid getting fired for doing something bizarre that was not in line with job policies and procedures, I decided to quit. I was not going to be one of those persons who didn't have time to plan or prepare, get fired unexpectedly and then left to figure out what to do. At any moment, your job can be made redundant or you can get fired. Having a job is like having a controlling boyfriend. He makes his girlfriend commit to making all kind of changes just to suit his personality or to make himself happy, and then later he still decides to dump her. She is no longer beneficial to him. So now, she's left to figure out what to do.

I remember having to see my grandmother go through such a hurtful and unplanned situation such as deployment. My grandmother had been working faithfully on a job for more than

30 years and one day when she least expected it, she was let go. She was faced with the decision to either go out and look for another job or create her own. It was either continue being an employee or become an entrepreneur. I am proud to say that grams bossed up. She used her talents and her skills and became an entrepreneur. My inspiration came from her bitter sweet experience. I decided to take ownership of my life and begin living in such a way that allowed me to be in full control of my own financial success.

It is my intent to continually push myself into being a risk taker, someone who is innovative, creative and seeks out those opportunities that allows my money to work for me.

I am now on a mission to motivate and inspire more people to take control of their lives. The world is filled with too much followers and not enough leaders, too much employees and not enough entrepreneurs.

This is no longer the traditional age. You don't have to follow or live your life based on traditional guidelines. The traditional guideline says: go to school, get good grades, graduate, attend college, look for a "good" or government job and then wait for retirement to really enjoy life. In my opinion, that plan and idea is out-dated. This is the information age where there are smarter and much easier ways to do everything. You could be earning millions of dollars without a college degree. I'm not saying don't go to college but I'm realizing that college isn't for everyone. A formal education may help you make a living, but self education, networking and the life and an entrepreneur can help you make a fortune.

Again, you don't even have to have some major business or company with hundreds or thousand of employees. The whole idea is to become someone who is determined, creative and innovative enough to create financial opportunities that provides a life of freedom. You should be using your spare time wisely, to read more, learn more, develop your skills, pursue your passions, create, invent or invest in something. You should be trying to find ways to create streams of income so that you could fire your job and your job won't have the chance to fire you.

As you know there are many successful entrepreneurs who either quit college or quit their jobs. They decided that they were not going to be labeled as employees. They decided that they were not going to prepare themselves to be controlled by the system. Instead, they decided that they were going to boss up, take control of their lives and determine their own economic and financial status. They decided that they were not cut out to be employee's. Examples are people like Steve Jobs, Co-founder of Apple. Michael Dell, Founder and Chief executive officer of Dell Computers. Sir Richard Branson, Founder of Virgin group of companies and Mark Zuckerberg, Co-founder and Chief executive officer of Facebook. These are people who followed their curiosity and are now enjoying the benefits.

There is a saying that says, "curiosity kill the cat." Well, in actuality curiosity is the thing that is creating more and more millionaires daily. So, in my opinion, it is great to follow your instincts and be curious about your potential to do something amazing. It is good sometimes to have that "what if"mind set. I'm sure if someone were to question those men about their life and the decisions they've made, they would proudly say that quitting college or their jobs were the best choice they've ever made in their lives. Today those same men are millionaires and billionaires. So, I'm pretty sure it was the best decision.

Maybe you are someone like me and you want to take ownership of your life the same way those guys did. You know within yourself that having a job is keeping you back or will keep you back from experiencing the unlimited freedom and opportunities that the universe is waiting to offer you. Well, I have one piece of advice for you. If you are currently employed and you are feeling that way, then it's time to plan your move of escape.

They say winners never quit and quitters never win, but it all depends on what you are quitting on. In this situation, you would be quitting on the biggest scam that has ever been created. You would be quitting on a system that is unpredictable and unsure. You would be choosing to become the master of your life, rather than settling to be the slave to a master. Don't feel bad. When you do decide to get rid of your job or decide not to apply for one at all you are choosing to win rather than choosing to lose time, freedom and unlimited opportunities.

After nine years, I realized that I had more to do with my life other than sit around hoping to get a raise, a good position or a better job. I realized that even the people with seemingly good jobs as society would rate it, hated going in to work every day or hated having a job, especially those government employees.

It is time for you to begin creating and doing things in your own unique way.

It's time for you to passionately follow those curious thoughts and feelings and allow that curiosity to lead you into a life of success and financial independence. You can either take control of you life now or end up being controlled by your job for the rest of your life. If no one has ever told you, I will be the first to tell you. You have the potential to become more than just someone's employee.

In this book, you will get see the many reasons why you may not be cut out to be an employee and why I concluded that I was not cut out to be one either. I truly believe that when you and I were created, we were created to be awesome, to be different and to be ourselves. Therefore when there is a desire to do more or become someone of a more meaningful existence, you should not settle.

This book will definitely inspire you!

YOU

ARE

MORE

THAN

JUST

SOMEONE'S

EMPLOYEE

DO NOT

SETTLE.

BE BOLD

BE BRAVE

TAKE

MORE

RISKS.

BELIEVE

IN

YOURSELF!

I AM TOO MUCH

A LITTLE BIT OF EVERYTHING

---

*It takes courage to grow up
and turn out to be who you
really are.*

~Edward Estlin Cummings~

What type of person are you? Well, me, I am
one of those persons who enjoy waking up
feeling like I've had sufficient rest. It is a
joy waking up knowing that I've slept well
and don't have to rush into a job that I don't
enjoy. Whenever I get up in the mornings, I
listen to calming piano or jazz instrumentals.
That sort of music puts me in a positive mood
and prepares me to begin my morning rituals.
Most days I start my mornings off by giving
thanks for all the many blessings and all the
people that are a part of my life. Then I begin
speaking positive affirmations over my life.
Once I'm relaxed, calm and in a good mood, I
am then able to start my day. Some mornings
when I get up, I am naturally hyped up and in

good spirits. I dance around my bed room to either pop, reggae or rap music for about twenty minutes. It is a form of meditation for me, and I love it. That is how I like to start my day. Whenever I can start my day like that, I am the most positive, energetic and nicest persons in the world. If I am not able to start my day doing any of those things, I can promise you, I won't be nice or normal. I'm like a coffee drinker who needs their morning coffee. A lot of coffee drinkers in the mornings are moody and won't talk or won't function properly until they get that coffee. I am the exact same way with my morning rituals. It's a must.

Most employees go to work complaining about almost everything and honestly, I can't deal with being around people like that all day, every day. Whenever I went into work, even though I didn't enjoy being there, I went in happy and in good spirits. I was always ready to enjoy my day. Some of my colleagues used to look at me as if I was some lunatic. I was just the guy who decided to be happy, positive and open minded about everything. Some people would probably say that I am schizophrenic, bipolar or just weird.

Whatever anyone thought or think, honestly, I am a little bit of everything, and I am cool with that. I learnt to fully embrace the person I've become. On the job that was an issue. Therefore, while I still had the chance, I decided to quit. I'm just not cut out to be an employee anyway.

Firstly, I am what you would call an ambivert. An AMBIVERT? I know you're thinking like gee, what is that? An ambivert is neither a full introvert or extrovert, but a little bit of both. Yes, I am a little bit of both. I do enjoy being in social gatherings around a lot of people and when I am, I am the life of the party, but I also enjoy my space, being alone sometimes. Not every day I am interested in communicating with a lot of people. I know you may be thinking, this is some weird dude. The reality is, there are a lot of people like myself. Honestly, there are times when I just need to recharge, refocus and make sure I am in the right frame of mind. Sometimes at my old job I wanted to snap at some people and to be honest, once or twice I did.I really didn't intend to. I am a nice guy, I just hate being bothered when I don't feel like being like being bothered. This was a major problem for me having a job.

Secondly, I think I may be in the primary stage of having ADHD. I'm certain that, if I were to visit a psychologist or someone else who studies the mind and human behavior they would diagnose me as one of those persons. My attention span is short, I am not very good at sitting down in one place for too long and I get hyper active sometimes and can't even control the feelings. I end up dancing around or doing something wild and fun. It's like a rush of energy and excitement overwhelms me. Many times, at my old job my colleagues thought I was being weird or acting crazy. I was simply being myself, but then again, that was a major problem. I just can't be in one place for too long. I need scenery. I need music. I need fresh air. I need to be free.

I guess that would explain the reason why I hate shoes so much. I am what you would call a bare feet island boy. I love my feet to be free. I'm certain that in a few years I'll be given the name "The bare feet rich guy or the bare feet millionaire."

In my opinion the best way to work is in slippers or with no shoes on at all. Well of course being in a professional environment or at most jobs you can't do that. That was a major issue for me. My colleagues sometimes would say to me that I was being unprofessional or behaving in an unethical way, but again, I was simply being myself.

The thing is you may not be as weird as I am or have all those weird conditions like I do. You may be a person who is just too good of a web designer, too good of a carpenter, too good of a comedian or actor, too good of a DJ, too good of a song writer, too good of a singer, too good of an event planner, too good of a makeup artist, too good of a photographer. You may be someone who is super sexy and extremely photogenic, maybe you need to become a model or something. Whatever it is, I'm pretty sure that you are too much a little bit of something to be settling and not focusing on building your own brand or business. I would hate to know that you go your entire life never completely being yourself and pursing the things that you are passionate about just to have and keep a job. You are just too awesome and too cool for your personality and creativity to be contained in a box. You should be out in the world doing you.

I am reminded of Russell Simmons book Do You. It's time to "DO YOU." Experience the freedom that you deserve. Don't settle to fit in and don't keep putting your dreams on hold.

I LOVE FREEDOM

Freedom! freedom! I can't move

Freedom, cut me loose!

Freedom! freedom! where are you?

Cause I need freedom too!

I break chains all by myself

Won't let my freedom rot in hell

Hey! Ima keep running cause a winner don't quit on themselves

~Beyoncé~

If I had stayed at my job or applied for another I would have been settling just like everybody else. Whenever you settle to live a life that you are not completely happy about, you are quitting on yourself. You are quitting on your dreams. You are giving up on your potential to become a better person and giving up on all the other financial opportunities that can help you to live a more meaningful life. Don't settle my friend.

At some point, we must all decide to take control of our lives. I stopped being afraid to quit a job because I realized that by being afraid I was limiting myself. I was watching so many other people enjoy life and I wasn't. That bothered me a lot. I figured that I should be out there exploring, being adventurous, traveling, making money easily and spending more time with the people I love. I couldn't deal with the idea of being stuck at a job working 8hours or more, making money that I knew could be made in much easier ways doing something that I truly love. I started being more excited about a lifestyle of freedom. I started thinking back to the days when I started a few small businesses of my own. There was no boss, no schedule, no rules and no regulations. I did whatever I wanted, whenever I wanted.

I didn't have to submit some vacation form and then cross my fingers hoping I get what I requested. I didn't have to explain anything to anyone. I didn't have anyone monitoring or supervising me, telling me what I should or shouldn't do. I decided to completely quit the job market and regain my freedom. In my opinion having a job is still slavery. It's just the modern-day kind of slavery with some perks and benefits to keep you going into work, helping you to forget about your dreams and aspirations.

Believe it or not but life is all about investing. You are always investing your time or money into something or someone. In this amazing world that some of us call home you will either be investing your time and freedom for money or you will be investing your money to have more time and more freedom.

There came a point where I began looking over and analyzing my life. I then realized that I was not really living and enjoying life. I was not traveling the way I wanted to and I wasn't doing the things that I preferred to be doing daily. My time and social life was being controlled by a job. Weekends off and vacation time was limited freedom. I was investing my time for money and I wasn't completely happy about it.

There will come a point in life where no matter how much money you earn you will always desire to have more time and more freedom. If all you do is work, work, work, you will never get a feeling of joy in doing that. You will desire to spend more time with friends and love ones. You will desire to have a more active social life and you will desire to have more freedom. Money is a great thing to have. It is a necessity in life, so we all need it, but instead of investing so much of my time and freedom to have it. I decided to use some of the money that I earned over the years and invest it in the things that I have interest in. I need my freedom.

Sometimes I sit down and think to myself how so many of us were taught from young to become employees. As a result, many of us became slaves to the system.
Majority of the people that have jobs spend

most of their time at work and by the time they get home, they are too tired to do anything. The only thing most employees do after work is eat, sleep and then prepare for work the next day. Do you know that a lot of people who have jobs hardly spend time with family or friends? They hardly have a social life and they hardly communicate with coworkers outside of work. Therefore, a lot of people who have jobs are just what the system want them to be. They are tired old slaves with no friends and no social life. Do you realize that having a job is one of the major reasons why some husbands and wives split? Both or one of them are always working. They are too busy for each other. Therefore, they grow apart, they lose that affection and before they realize it, the romance in the relationship is gone. One of them are always too tired to do something with or for the other. This is why some kids hardly have close bonds with their parents. The kids are at school all day and the parents are at work all the time. This is also the reason why there are only few families now that sit down at the table with each other at the end of the day to have a meal and talk about their day. Why? Well, because nobody has the time. Everyone is just too busy or too tired.

My advice to anyone who truly wants to experience a life of freedom, is to spend more time working on your dreams than you spend working for your job. You owe it to yourself to live life your way. Having freedom should be a big deal for you. Even if it's not the kind of freedom that allows you to travel every weekend or every month, you should still desire the kind of freedom that allows you to make your own rules. It's your life, right? Boss up for god sake.

I could remember some time ago I was driving on the road and a lady almost hit my car. I didn't over react. I simply honked my horn to alert her that she was about to hit my car and then drove off after she didn't. You and I both know if someone was to almost hit your car on the street because of their reckless driving you would either give them the finger, verbally curse at them or follow them while honking your horn just to argue. In most cases, people end up doing all of the above. We make a big deal in situations like that, but in a situation like that, I won't. Now, anytime someone parks a vehicle in the front of my vehicle, blocking me in, I get highly upset and immediately over react. I hate feeling trapped. Even to this day I would not park my car in a place where I feel as if someone is going to block me in. I would freak out. The only place I don't mind being blocked in is on an airplane, put me by the window seat and I'm be cool. On an airplane, there are not much places to go anyway, so it won't be a problem, but the second I notice a vehicle blocking my vehicle, Huston we will have a problem.

You may be thinking that's not a great illustration to explain how much I love freedom, but trust me it is. As simple as someone blocking my vehicle is a big deal to me. Imagine spending eight hours a day on a job doing what someone else wanted me to do and not being able to do what I wanted. I felt trapped and I believe so many people feel that exact same way, but I can now do the things I love and enjoy doing. I have full control over my day and I determine what kind of people I spend time with.

Imagine this for a moment. Imagine an evening out with fun, amazing friends and family. Everyone bursting with positive energy. The food is great, the drinks are on point and as the millennial's like to say the music was "lit" it is just the kind of excitement that you needed in your life. You are having so much fun and you wish the night could go on forever, but you drank a little too much, so you must leave. Arriving home safely, you hit the bed whole-sail, (clothes still on). The only thing you manage to do is remove your shoes. The next day you wake up with a smile on your face stretching your arms out wide, from left to right. You're feeling great. You didn't have to wake up to the sound of an annoying alarm clock, reminding you that it's time to go to the people job. You were awakened naturally. You were not forced to get up, you didn't have to rush to get ready and you didn't have to call anyone explaining that you would be arriving late. There is no schedule and no boss. Isn't that a sweet life to have? It sure is, but it doesn't have to be just an imagination. It can be your reality.

My friend, don't settle to live a life your parents or teachers want you to live. Live a life that makes you excited everyday to wake up to, a life that makes you happy. Live a life that you aren't forced to live, but force yourself to live the life that you wish to have. I am in love with freedom, how about you?

I PREFER, FIRST NAMES

&

HANDSHAKES

In my opinion, a lot of people are just too formal to be normal. Me on the other hand, I am just too normal to be formal. I am the cool guy. I honestly hate feeling as if I'm in the military, having to address everyone as sir and mam or mister and mistress all the time. I'm not a disrespectful guy, I just prefer addressing someone by their first name without all the formal colonial stuff.

I remember growing up as a kid I couldn't even call my own aunts and uncles by their first names without saying aunty or uncle. If I did I probably would've gotten a beating. In The Bahamas where I'm from, It is known as total disrespect to address a stranger by their first name, especially if the person is older or has a prestige position or title. If you do, it is said that you are no manners or out of order, you will definitely get the side eye.

On the last job where I worked as a security officer, it was known as "respect" on the job to address people as mister or mistress or to call them by their last name. I hated that so much. I could remember meeting this very cool wealthy guy. I always addressed him as mister. One day he decided to stop and have a conversation. He reached out his hand to shake mine, so in return I extended my hand to shake his. He asked, "Young man what is your name?" I replied, "My name is Rashad." He said to me, "Rashad, please, whenever you see me just call me Jerry." At that very moment, I felt so relieved. I honestly preferred calling him by his first name anyway. I prefer calling everybody by their first name, it's just my way. Anyway, every time after that I was always so happy to see him and call him Jerry.

They say if you don't know a man call him mister, but I say if you don't know a man go over, start a conversation, introduce yourself, smile, reach your hand out for a handshake and get to know his name. Introducing yourself and getting to know someone's first name gives you an opportunity to possibly meet your soul mate, business partner or just a good friend.

If you were to look at some of the world most successful men like Mark Zuckerberg and Richard Branson you would notice that these guys do everything differently from how society expects it to be done. Those guys are game changers. Richard Branson is one of those entrepreneurs who I admire for his free spirit and positive attitude toward life. If you were to ever follow any of them around their offices you probably won't even notice who's the boss. They dress casually and they walk around the office interacting with their employees as if they are one themselves. It is a strategy that successful entrepreneurs use called "breaking corporate hierarchy barriers." It is a strategy where you create an environment without any feelings of separation between the boss and the employee. No one is superior or inferior. It's all about equality. I love being in those kinds of environments. Everybody is just so chill, nobody cares about addressing anyone in a formal way. In environments and around people like that, people are more concerned about how productive or successful you are at whatever you do, and to me that's cool. I'm pretty sure if one of Mark or Richard employees were to call them by their first name, which a lot of them probably already do, it wouldn't be a big deal to them.

On the last job where I work as a security at a hotel, I can recall the time when I worked alongside one of the guys who at the time were a security director. Him and I had been working together on a special assignment assisting some of the hotel guests. While walking in route to assist the guests, him an I walked about four feet away from each other. I needed to get his attention so I called him by his first name. I called his name about 3 or 4 times and he never answered. Again, he was only a 4ft distance away from me. I knew he could hear me. He wasn't deaf. It wasn't until I used the term mister and addressed him by his last name, he decided to answer. I was shocked to know that he literally did not answer me because I chose not to address him by his last name using the term mister. I was highly upset but didn't show it at that time. We finally arrived to assist the ladies who were guest of the hotel.

In route to our destination the ladies freely called him by his first name the entire time. He was laughing and enjoying the conversation as they were making jokes. I stopped and paused for a second, placed both hands on my waist, looked up in the sky and rolled my eyes. I began thinking to myself, "this guy can't be serious, what is his problem?" The ladies stopped, looked back and asked me if everything was okay. I replied, "oh yes, it's nothing, everything is fine." I couldn't believe it. I also thought to myself, what if I wasn't an employee and he wasn't one of my bosses, it wouldn't have been a problem me calling him by his first name. I was pissed, but to avoid any back and forward debating or arguing I just stayed calm and addressed him as mister.

To be called by your first name in my opinion is an honor. Why wouldn't it be? For example, if you were given the name Mike as a child and your parents called you Mike your entire life, I don't understand how or why would it be disrespectful for someone to call you Mike. It's your name for goodness sake. First names and handshakes are my preferred way of meeting and greeting people. All that mister, mistress, colonial and formal greeting isn't my kind of thing. Even if I were to ever go out and find another job that has a first name and hand shake policy which I'm sure some jobs do, I still would find something else to hate and be pissed off about on that job. So instead of me being pissed off or coming off as disrespectful on a job. I decided to quit the job market. I concluded that, I'm just not cut out to be an employee. I rather be out in the world enjoying my freedom, doing things my way. I prefer first names and handshakes, what about you?

I AM A LAZY INTELLIGENT

The simpler it is, the better I like it

~Peter Lynch~

Before you get it all twisted, a lazy intelligent is not really a lazy person. A lazy intelligent is someone who works differently. In fact, the term lazy intelligent is a type of mindset and work ethic. Lazy intelligent's are people like: Warren Buffet, Steve Jobs, Bill Gates, Sir Richard Branson, Robert Kiyosaki, Marc Fisher, Timothy Ferriss oh and I can't forget the guys who came up with the idea for Uber. Garret Camp and Travis Kalanick. Those guys are making millions from using their employee's vehicles to run their taxi service company. Those guys are the real deal examples of what the lifestyle of a lazy intelligent looks like. The way those people live and earn their money, the average person would say, "they're lazy and they don't know the value of hard work."

Well that's the point, they were clever enough to find out how not to work so hard. They believed in themselves, they invested in something that they were passionate about and now they don't have to physically work hard. Their employees and their money work for them. You probably don't know it yet or haven't tapped into that side of you yet, but the reality is, YOU have the potential and the ideas of a lazy intelligent.

A lazy intelligent is an Actionaire, someone who takes smart actions. A lazy intelligent is someone who believes in the principle of working smart and not hard. Lazy intelligent's are creative thinkers. Most lazy intelligent's believe strongly in the power of an idea, in the power of networking or in the power of investing. Most importantly they believe in themselves. They use their gifts, skills and talents to the best of their ability and take full advantage of all the resources provided, to make their dreams a reality. Most lazy intelligent's surround themselves with people who are most of the time smarter than they are or know a lot more people than they do.

A lazy intelligent is not selfish and is someone who understands the power of partnership. Many years ago, before we even heard or knew about Facebook, Mark Zuckerberg invited 5 people to his Harvard dorm room to discuss a business opportunity. Out of the 5 people who he invited, it is said that only 2 of those persons showed up. Today Dustin Moskovitz and Eduardo Saverin are billionaires. Some of the reasons why some people never experience the success that they are imagining or hoping to experience is because of greed, selfishness, failure to network and sometimes overlooking the idea to partner up with something or someone. Don't be the one to miss out.

On the cover of his book The Lazy Millionaire, Marc Fisher has a quote by Leonardo da Vinci and it says "Geniuses often accomplish more when they work less." This is a proven fact. If you were to Google the names of some of the world's most successful business men and women, you would find out that they are the ones with the major companies known worldwide. While thousands of employees work for them, they are somewhere playing tennis, playing golf, out riding on a yacht or at home in a robe, pajamas and bed room slippers. WORK SMART AND NOT HARD is something I truly believe in.

I remember back at one of my jobs, I always heard my colleagues say stuff like: "I'd rather be tired than broke." Whenever I heard that, my eyebrows always raised. I never enjoyed being tired and I never believed in working more hours than I had to. Therefore, I totally disagreed with that statement. Most rich or wealthy people are the ones who put in less hours and make a lot more money than the people busting their hip on some job. They understand the principle, work smart and not hard. I could remember some time back my sister and I talked about her college friends. She mentioned to me that some of them were really care free and did a lot of partying. She said to me that she noticed for some reason that they were the ones to always get the good grades. I explained to her that the reason they could succeed like that was because, they were not over studying or over working their brain.

Therefore, when it was time to remember something, their minds were free enough to reveal to them all the things they needed to succeed. I have this quote I like to remind myself of, "If you study long, you will study wrong." Trust me, this is something I have proven and I'm sure you can relate.

Napoleon Hill wrote a book called "Think and Grow Rich." The name of that book had and still has many readers intrigued. It has been on the best sellers list for years. Napoleon was one of those persons who understood spiritual laws and principles. He understood how the mind works. He understood that science and spirituality all go hand in hand. He knew that energy, vibration, thought and words are all languages of the universe, and all play a part in manifesting negative or positive experiences in one's life. Majority of the wealthiest people understand the mind power and they understand laws and principles. That is the reason why they are always progressing and succeeding in life. If you are unaware of how the mind functions and how to make use of certain laws and principles, you will never live a productive and successful life. In my other eBook "The key to success is your mind" you will see just how powerful your mind is and how you can change everything about your life and get the results that you need through the power of the mind.

I want you to know that it is okay to think like a lazy intelligent, to have the attitude of one or aspire to live that lifestyle. The world need your creativity. Therefore, it is time to get your intelligent, super talented, extremely creative butt out there and begin creating and inventing things that can change the world and of course your financial status. Don't settle to be just another employee, become and live like a LAZY INTELLIGENT! Lazy intelligent's are some of the world's greatest inventors, authors, designers, photographers, painters, musicians, app makers, entrepreneurs and the list goes on. You can be one to. There are many people who became millionaires and billionaires the lazy intelligent way. They came up with brilliant ideas, got investors to come on board, hired the necessary persons and then made their dreams come alive. Some people didn't even need investors, they just came up with some brilliant idea and then worked consistently to produce the most effective service and or products that attracted the masses.

There are many businesses, inventions, books, designs, talents, skills and creativity on the inside of you, but if you spend most of your time overworking on some job you will never enjoy the lifestyle of a lazy intelligent. Most of the time all it takes is one idea. One idea can make you millions or even billions. It's all a matter of being innovative, creative, consistent and believing in yourself.

I AM TOO CREATIVE

&

ENTREPRENEUR MINDED

It doesn't matter who you are, entrepreneurship boils down to having a good idea and being resourceful enough to turn it into a reality.

~Sir Richard Branson~

In the era in which we live, if you can properly brand and market yourself, market your product and or services and build a social media following you can generate a lot of traffic/viewers and by networking you can turn lurkers into customers and the result is, you make money. That is one way of being resourceful.

You are reading the book of someone who has always been determined to do something creative and be unchained from a desk and from working at some job. I did many creative and innovative things and my intent is to continue. I've had an auto detailing business. I've had partnership in a food take away stand. I've produced and sold my own flavored drinks with the help of some family. I made a lot of money very quickly in that venture. During those hot summer months when I knew everybody needed ice cold beverages, my team and I stood in the middle of traffic and made sure every person stuck in traffic got one of our icy cold beverages. I've established an after-partying cleaning business and I've printed and sold motivational t-shirts with the slogan "I'm all about that Faith, bout that Faith No $truggle." I just want to keep creating. As you read this book right now I am probably thinking about the next creative idea to add to my portfolio. My daily slogan is "money gotta make" When you are entrepreneur minded, it's hard to just give up and throw in the towel. Some of my business ventures may not have gone as planned but I never allowed that to stop me. Whenever you decide to become a freelancer or an entrepreneur, some of your ventures may end up an EPIC failure but that doesn't mean that you failed. When making attempts to create the light bulb Thomas Edison said "I have not failed, I just found ten thousand ways that didn't work." I can truly say that being on this entrepreneurial journey I found a lot of things that didn't work but my knowledge increased, and I became more and more passionate about being my own boss. Have you ever thought about doing anything for yourself? Have you ever had an idea that you know could possibly be turned into an income? Have you ever thought about being your own boss or being someone else's boss with your own business or company? Have you ever even imagined just making money from the comfort of your home? Well all those things are possible. The main goal should be to take more risks, be more curious and be more creative. Allow your life to spiral into a world of creativity and endless opportunities. These days you can literally make money doing anything and I mean anything.

You can get into real estate investing, buying and selling, flipping homes and properties. I know for sure that is my next big move. You can become an affiliate marketer, a network marketer, a digital marketer, an eBook writer, a fashion blogger, a food blogger, a lifestyle blogger, a photographer or even an investor in the financial markets. You can start an online store through drop shipping and Shopify selling anything and not even have to personally deal with shipping and inventory yourself. You can create your own clothing line and print catchy slogans on tee shirts and have thousands and millions of people wear your brand. Nike did it, so, why can't you?

The money opportunities are endless. Another financial opportunity that seems to be trending lately is something call cryptocurrency/digital currency investing. One of the currencies is called Bitcoin. Bitcoin is a decentralized currency meaning that banks have no control. It cannot be stopped or seized. Bitcoin has already made a few millionaires over the years. When I first heard of Bitcoin, the value of it was about $200. I didn't have any understanding of it.

Through networking I began hearing more about it. During the time of writing this book the value of bitcoin went up to about $1500 and the value of it still seems to be increasing. Millionaires and Billionaires like Richard Branson and Bill Gates have also invested in bitcoin. It is said that bitcoin could be worth 1 million dollars at some point. Well, I've invested a few bucks, I'm not rich but my investment has certainly increased. There are many financial opportunities for you to consider.

There is always another level of boss you can work your way up to. The grind never stops and the hustle must continue. Just how there is more than enough air for all of us to breathe, there is certainly more than enough money for everyone of us to make millions. I don't care how much governments declare a financial deficit or a recession, money doesn't go any where. There is no lack of it and honestly there can never be a lack of it. We can all have some riches. Therefore you must never underestimate the power of the Internet, the power of networking, the power of investing and never underestimate your potential. Any and everything is possible and there is no such thing as a such a stupid idea.

A lady by the name of Roni Di Lullo literally made millions by selling sun glasses for dogs. You may be thinking, sun glasses for dogs, really? Yes really. It may seem stupid but the lady is making money baby.

Tim Stone is a guy who left his job as a welder working for a major welding company to literally remove dog poop from people's yard. Come on Tim, isn't there anything else to do? you may ask. Yes, there are plenty things Tim could have done but he decided to remove dog poop from people yard, and he is making thousands of dollars a month from doing it.

If it is an idea that can make you money to enjoy a life of freedom then go ahead, do it, create it, launch it, build it. Do whatever it takes to make it happen. What you must know is that your idea or business doesn't even have to be original. It can be someone else's idea, but you must know how to be a lot more creative with the idea than the person who it originated from.

I'm not sure who came up with the idea to produce yoga mats but I know it was a completely other person or company who did the same thing but made the yoga mats a little longer and a little wider and they too made millions from that. You must keep thinking creatively my friend.

If you are an employee, could you imagine getting fired today or tomorrow? I know you can't. The thing is, those jobs won't always give you a chance to plan and prepare. At your job, you could say the wrong thing, a hateful minded or jealous colleague could come up with some false accusation that is totally believable and before you know it, you are out of there, stuff happens. The wrong move and you are out. Your job doesn't care about your mortgage, your rent, your car note, neither your college loan. All your job cares about is that you show up and do whatever the hell they tell you to do, and come to think, people are committed to their jobs more than they are to their dreams. WOW. It is time for you to begin believing in your dreams. Instead of settling for a limited income and a boring social life, put on your creative cap and become a part of the entrepreneurial world. The world of creative geniuses. When you are an entrepreneur you are actually the architect of your future. You can design your life the way you desire. The government may change, policies and procedures may change but you my friend can create your own economy.

This is not a coincidence and certainly it is not a mistake that you are reading this book at this point in your life.

The famous Bahamian author, Dr. Myles Munroe, before he died said that when a person dies they should die empty. He said that when and individual goes to the grave, they should have done everything they needed and wanted to do. He also said that the wealthiest place in the world is the cemetery. The reason he considered the cemetery to be the wealthiest place was because in the cemetery he said "there are books that were never written, music that were never heard, paintings that we've never seen, poetry that has never been read, businesses that has never been opened, companies that has never been started and inventions that we have never used." People took to the grave with them many gifts and talents that the world may never know of. They died poor with rich ideas. They allowed someone to talk them out of their dreams. They allowed fear to box them in or they made excuses and underestimated themselves.

Imagine if the people who invented vehicles, telephones, televisions and airplanes would have just talked about their dreams and never put together a plan and then act. We probably would not have been enjoying all this luxury and convenience that we have today. I'm pretty sure that some of them did many things and wasn't successful in some ventures. Some of them probably didn't even have sufficient funding or didn't have any funding at all but like any real entrepreneur minded individual, they had to be resourceful and creative to make stuff happen.

I remember the first business I started. I didn't have a lot of funding to successfully start, but in my mind, I knew that I would find a way to make it all happen. This is where I had to now be resourceful. I bossed up. I knew I wanted a set location with a nicely built car port to detail vehicles, but firstly I had to think of ways to generate more money to successfully launch. I knew I needed a truck. I needed top of the line cleaning products and I needed people to help me in detailing vehicles. I realized I needed a lot of things but didn't have a lot money. I didn't allow that to stop me. My uncle had a truck. I put my pride aside and allowed my passion and determination to drive me. I shared my idea with him and confidently asked him to invest in my idea by loaning me his truck. He said yes. At that point, I realized I could use his truck to start doing mobile detailing and that would help me to accumulate the money I needed. As soon as I came up with the idea I went into work the next week an resigned effective immediately. I knew I was supposed to give a two weeks' notice but I was too excited. I had finally come up with a business idea. During that same week of resigning I called one of my friends who I knew at the time didn't have any work and he became my first business partner, not legally but he was the guy I started out with.

Together we were the best. That same year December 2010, my family had planned a trip and decided to take me along with them. While on the trip my uncle received a call from a friend of his asking him if he knew anyone who was interested in running a car wash. While talking on the phone, my uncle called me over and asked if I was interested in running my own stationary car wash. It was exactly what I wanted. I was extremely excited and said yes. What was so amazing, even though at that point I had made enough money to purchase all the things I needed to run a successful auto detailing business, I never had to use my own money to pay for anything. I was resourceful and took initiative. As a result everything and every person that I needed was made available for me. I can truly say that the universe had my back. My uncle's wife heard the news, and her being a business woman herself, she was excited to invest financially into my business. It was more than a dream come through for me. My uncle and cousin built a nice carport. I got a three months supply of cleaning products from a friend of my uncle. It was everything I needed. Honestly, I never expected things to play out as good as they did, but they did. It was all because I never allowed fear to keep me in a box and I never made up excuses.

If it's one thing that I learned that you should know, in life there will never be a perfect time to do anything, but there will always be a right time to do something, and the right time to do anything is right now. I won't encourage you to become an entrepreneur or pursue your dreams only for the money, but you should at least be out there creating and seeking out those opportunities that will afford you a freer and relax lifestyle. If you are depending on a job for financial independence, you are making a big mistake.

If you consider yourself to be an entrepreneur minded individual but currently working on a job, there are some questions that you should be asking yourself. Questions like: what am I still doing here? Am I mentally and emotionally strong enough to deal with the situation of possibly not having a sure flow of income for a while? Do I have enough money to sustain me if I decide to quit my job? Do I have a plan?

Am I still here because I am trying to accumulate more funds or am I still here because I am afraid to step out and do what my heart really feels? These are a few simple but convicting questions you must ask yourself. A real entrepreneur minded individual will not settle year after year working on some job. Entrepreneur minded individuals know that they can always do a lot better and accomplish a lot more in the business world, doing something that they are passionate about.

Below are the names of some more, bold, brave, entrepreneur minded, risk takers. I'm sure there stories will inspire you.

Shep and Ian Murray are brothers who quit their jobs within ten minutes of each other. Shep was an advertising account executive and Ian worked at a small public relations firm. Despite being told how "dumb" their idea was, Shep and Ian started a tie company called Vineyard Vines. The brothers like to say that they traded in their business suits for bathing suits and started selling ties so that they don't have to wear them.

Shep and Ian are my kind of guys.

Rocky Patel quit his job as an Hollywood entertainment lawyer and decided to manufacture his own brand of cigars. Patel decided to tun his passion into an income. His friends and colleagues warned him against leaving his lucrative practice for an industry he didn't know anything about. Patel saw an opportunity to create a product that he knew the market needed. Therefore, he left the law business behind and began manufacturing cigars. Rocky Patel cigar now produces 20,000,000 cigars annually and in 2011 there were an estimated amount of 40 million dollars in sales. Now that, is being entrepreneur minded.

Surabhi Jain an Indian woman, once and employee at Google. If you know anything about working at Google you would know that Google employees really don't have to spend their money. Everything they need is provided to them on campus. You would wonder, why in the world would this woman quit? Well Surabhi was making a lot of money but she realized she wasn't happy and wasn't enjoying her life. So yes, she quit her "good Job" and went on to become a dancer. You may think that's crazy, a dancer, really? Yes really, she said, the transition has made her life a lot more balanced and happier.

Twenty eight year old Susie Romans, for years had been managing social media sites for small local businesses on a retainer of about $350 a month. She realized based on her connections in the business community and with her expertise in sales and marketing, she knew she could sign some clients on her own as a consultant. Romans remembers her friends and coworkers saying she was delusional to quit a "good" steady job. Late spring 2014, she pulled the plug on her day job. She knew that she could be earning more. She had two kids and a mortgage to pay, but she didn't allow that to stop her. She followed her curiosity and her passion, and she made the decision to quit. Her along with all those other individuals are now reaping and enjoying the benefits of taking risks.

Quitting a job or deciding not to get one in the first place won't be easy, I won't lie. Someone is going to try to talk you out of it. You will start to second guess your decisions, but, you can't allow yourself to be lured into the next 10 to 20 years of mediocre living. YOU! have a bigger purpose in life.

Trust me, there are hundreds, thousands and even millions of people waiting on a new business, a new service, a new product or for someone to come up with a new invention. You could be that someone. Don't end up 5 or 10 years from now regretting you didn't follow your heart and take the chance to live life on your own terms.

Remember, right now is the oldest you've ever been and the youngest you will ever be. So, it's time you stop being afraid and start doing things that are life changing, because YOU! yes you, YOU are more than just someone's employee.

LET'S GET IT, NOW LET'S GO!

www.ingramcontent.com/pod-product-compliance
Lightning Source LLC
Chambersburg PA
CBHW051243170526
45165CB00004B/1555